ANASTASIA

ANASTASIA

The Story

A magical mix of music, adventure, romance and comedy, **Anastasia** is a spectacular, full-length animated motion picture about the lost Russian princess, rumored to be the last surviving member of the Romanov family. One of the greatest mysteries of our time is brought to life in this unique twentieth-century fairy tale.

Life was a paradise for 8-year-old Princess Anastasia, living in the czar's palace in Russia with her family. But all that comes to an end one evening when the evil magician Rasputin appears, placing a curse on the entire royal family. Rasputin's curse comes true later that night when a mob storms the palace, beginning the Russian Revolution. With the help of Dimitri, a young palace servant, Anastasia and her beloved grandmother, Marie, escape. Marie manages to climb aboard a train to Paris, but Anastasia is swept up amongst the confusion and left behind. All Anastasia has left of her grandmother is a key to the music box she gave her, inscribed with a promise that someday they would be together in Marie's home in Paris.

It is now ten years after the fall of the Russian empire. An 18-year-old Russian girl named Anya stumbles into a charming con man named Dimitri. He convinces Anya that she could be the Princess Anastasia and should accompany him to Paris to claim her royal heritage. What Anya does not know is that Dimitri has the lost music box that belonged to Anastasia, and he is looking for a girl to pretend to be the princess. With the music box and a worthy imposter he hopes to convince Marie that he has found the Princess, and collect a large reward. Wishing to find her true identity, Anya sets off to Paris with Dimitri, an ex-aristocrat named Vladimir and a lovable dog, Pooka.

Contents

Anastasia

Anastasia is a willful and determined 18-year-old orphan, driven to overcome the loss of her childhood memories and eager to discover the truth about her past. Audiences will respond to her emotional goal of finding the family to which she belongs. Used to fighting her own battles, this fiery young woman is never afraid to say what's on her mind. Whether leaping to safety from a runaway train, mastering the intricacies of royal behavior, or going up against the supernatural powers of Rasputin, Anastasia is always up to the task that will realize her dream — to find her home.

Dimitri

Dimitri is a slick and scheming young con man whose desire to gain money covers his emotional need to be accepted, to no longer be on the outside looking in. As his hidden feelings for Anastasia grow, Dimitri stubbornly tries to hold on to his belief that money is everything. But even this schemer crumbles under love's spell. Dimitri changes from a con man who only thinks of himself to a young man who will sacrifice anything — the promise of money, even his own romantic hopes — to see that happiness comes to Anastasia, the woman he loves.

Marie

Matriarch of the royal Romanov family and Anastasia's loving grandmother, Marie in many ways represents the emotional center of the movie. Just as she gives up hoping she'll ever be reunited with her granddaughter, Marie is forced to once more expose her heart to potential disappointment. And once she has found Anastasia, Marie exhibits extraordinary strength.

Rasputin

The evil sorcerer Rasputin is trapped in a hellish limbo because of his unfulfilled curse against the Romanov family. Shocked to hear that Anastasia, the last surviving member of the family, is still alive after so many years, he vows to find her. Despite his nefarious intentions, Rasputin is a wildly comic character. With his manic mood swings and comic self-obsession, he emerges as a fresh twist to the traditional animated villain.

Bartok

Bartok is a comical albino bat, master of the droll comeback. The fast-flying, droll night creature is never at a loss for words, even if he only mutters them behind Rasputin's back. Bartok is a reluctant accomplice to his evil master's schemes, and, even though his little bat-body bears the brunt of the madman's mayhem, he accepts his fate philosophically.

Vladimir

Vladimir is a former aristocrat, cast off the opulent Russian Empire. With his charming manners, He uses his knowledge of the Russian Court to train Anastasia in the royal ways of a princess. The good-natured, kind-hearted Vladimir is an incurable romantic, and is the first to recognize and sanction the growing attraction between Anastasia and Dimitri.

Sophie

Sophie is first cousin and lady-in-waiting to the Dowager Empress Marie, Anastasia's grandmother. Sophie is the eternal optimist, and her ample charms are the targets of Vladimir's affection. She holds out hope against all odds that the real Anastasia will someday be found. At the same time, she respects Marie's feelings and knows she must protect them.

" Have You Heard ?

There's A Rumor In St. Petersburg! "

A Rumor In St. Petersburg

Lyrics by LYNN AHRENS

Music by STEPHEN FLAHERTY

A Rumor in St. Petersburg - 11 - 1
0090B

8

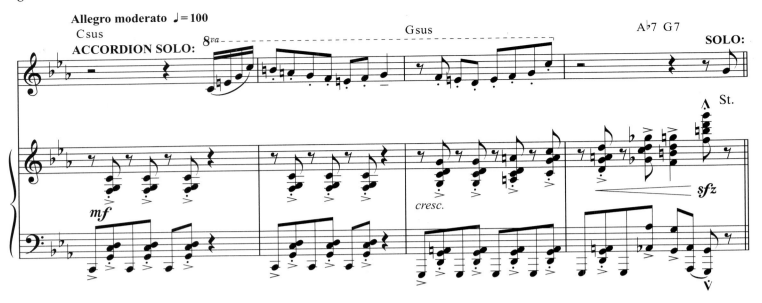

Pe-ters-burg is gloom-y. St. Pe-ters-burg is bleak! My un-der-wear got fro-zen stand-ing

here all week! Oh, since the rev-o-lu-tion, our lives have been so gray! Thank

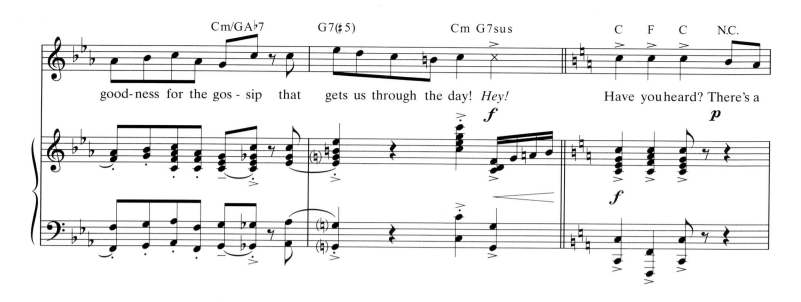

good-ness for the gos-sip that gets us through the day! *Hey!* Have you heard? There's a

ru-mor in St. Pe-ters-burg! Have you heard what they're say-ing on the street?! Al -

though the Tsar did not sur-vive, one daugh-ter may be still a-live! The

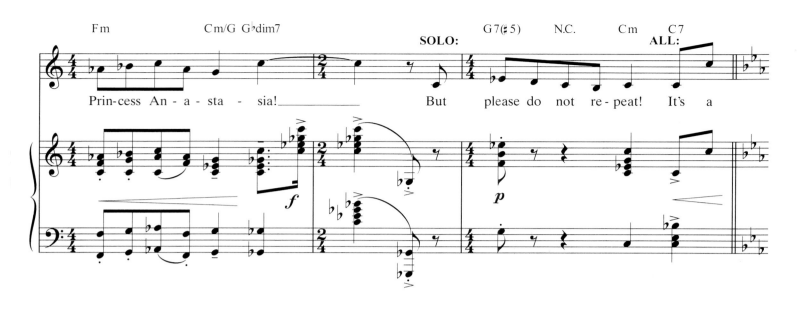

Prin-cess An-a-sta-sia!_____ But please do not re-peat! It's a

ru-mor, a leg-end, a mys-ter-y! Some-thing whis-pered in an al-ley-way or

through a crack! It's a ru-mor that's part of our his-to-ry! They

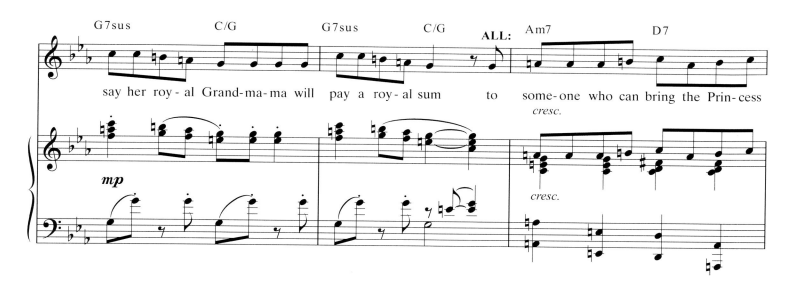

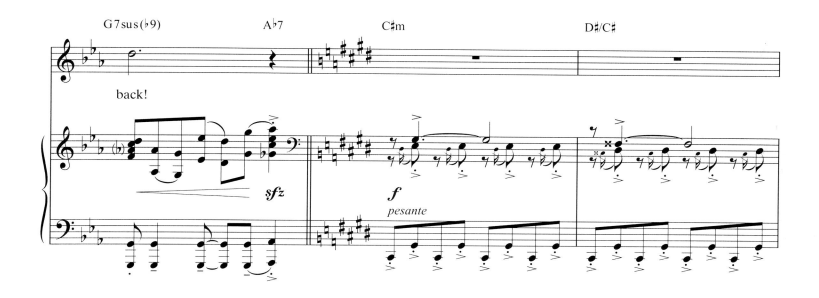

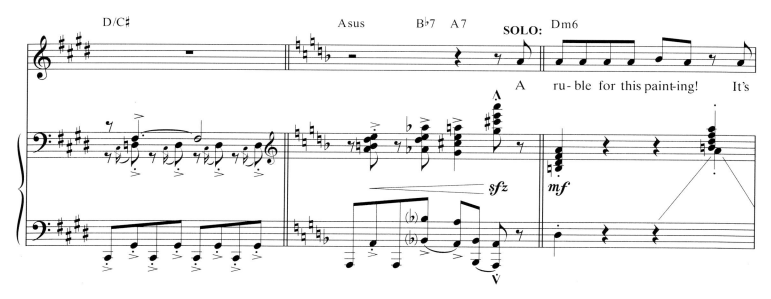

12

*Bracketed measures are not played on original recording.

A Rumor in St. Petersburg - 11 - 6
0090B

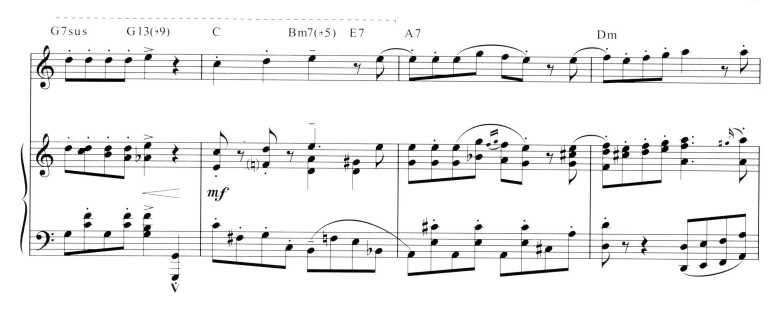

DIMITRI:

It's the

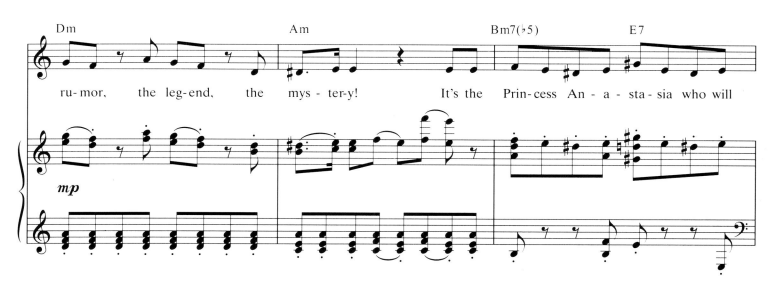

ru- mor, the leg-end, the mys- ter-y! It's the Prin-cess An - a - sta - sia who will

help us fly! You and I, friend, will go down in his-to-ry! We'll

find a girl to play the part and teach her what to say, dress her up and take her to "Pa-

ree!" Im - a - gine the re-ward her dear old Grand-ma-ma will pay! Who

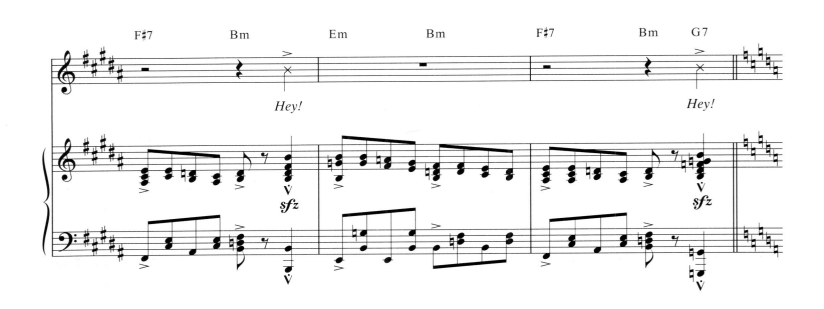

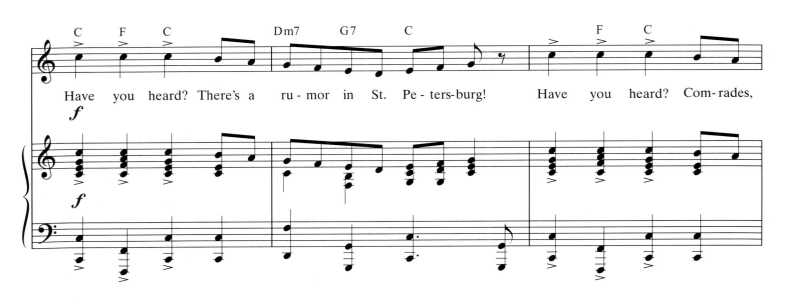

what do you sup-pose? A fas-ci-nat-ing mys-ter-y! The big-gest con in his-to-ry!___

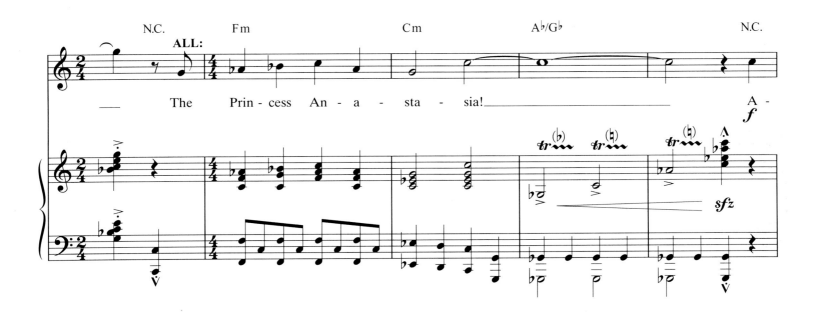

The Prin-cess An-a-sta-sia!_____ A-

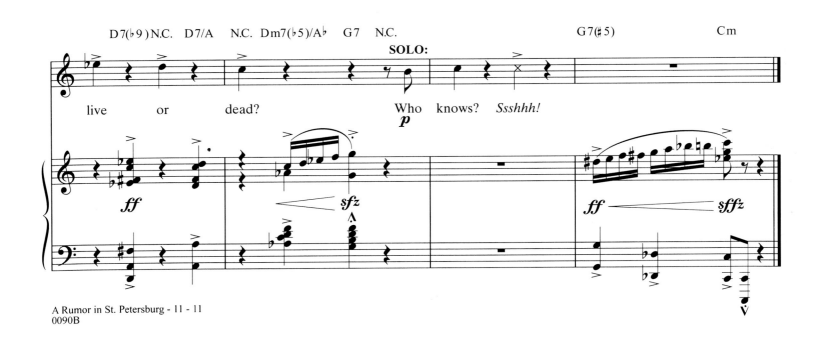

live or dead? Who knows? *Ssshhh!*

"I'll Be Safe And Wanted,

Finally Home Where I Belong.

Well, Starting Now, I'm Learning Fast,

On This Journey To The Past."

Journey To The Past

Lyrics by LYNN AHRENS

Music by STEPHEN FLAHERTY

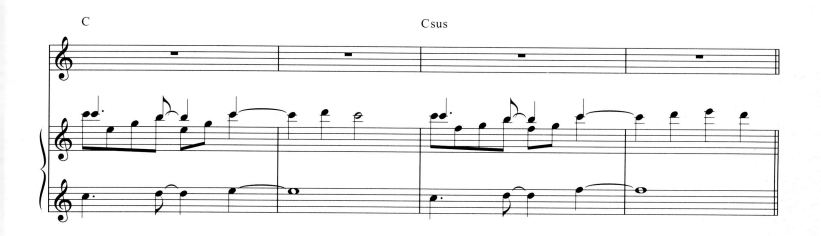

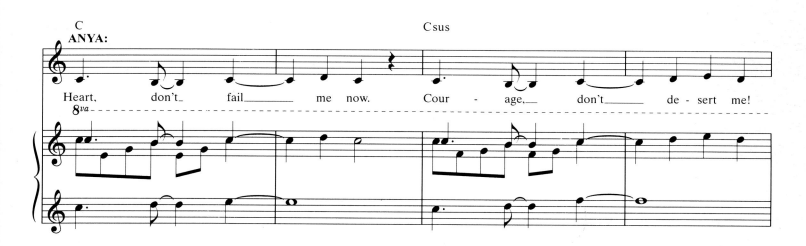

Journey to the Past - 8 - 1
0090B

"Dancing Bears, Painted Wings,

Things I Almost Remember.

And A Song Someone Sings

Once Upon A December."

Once Upon A December

Lyrics by LYNN AHRENS

Music by STEPHEN FLAHERTY

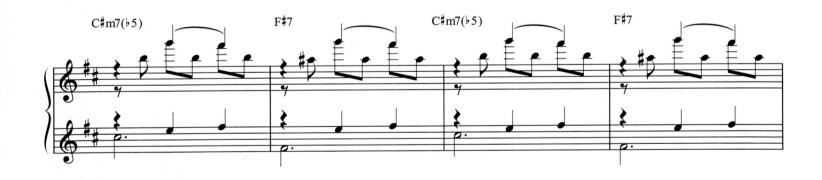

Once Upon a December - 7 - 1
0090B

Once Upon a December - 7 - 6
0090B

"In The Dark Of The Night,

Terror Will Strike Her!

In The Dark Of The Night

Evil Will Brew!"

In The Dark Of The Night

Lyrics by LYNN AHRENS

Music by STEPHEN FLAHERTY

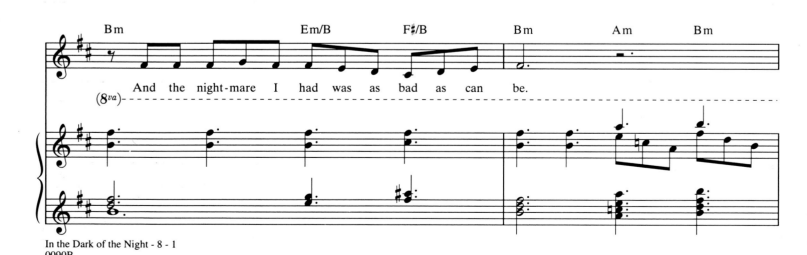

In the Dark of the Night - 8 - 1
0090B

38

In the Dark of the Night - 8 - 3
0090B

In the Dark of the Night - 8 - 8
0090B

"TELL YOURSELF IT'S EASY AND IT'S TRUE!

YOU CAN LEARN TO DO IT, TOO!"

Learn To Do It

Lyrics by LYNN AHRENS

Music by STEPHEN FLAHERTY

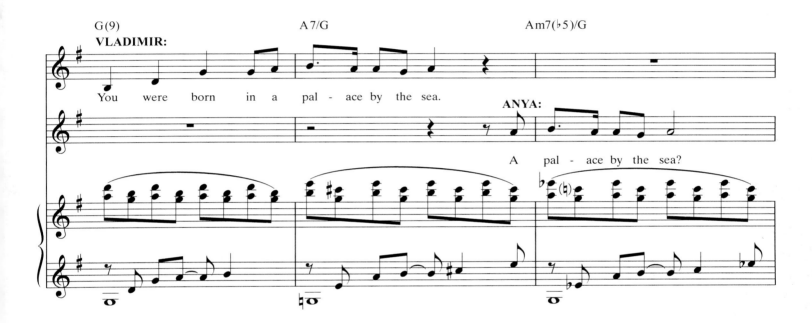

Learn To Do It - 9 - 1
0090B

"I'll Show You That French Joie De Vivre!

Paris Holds The Key To Your Heart.

And All Of Paris Plays A Part."

Paris Holds The Key
(To Your Heart)

Lyrics by LYNN AHRENS

Music by STEPHEN FLAHERTY

* Pronounced "Par-ee" throughout.

Paris Holds the Key - 11 - 1
0090B

Here, have a flow-er on me. For - get where you're from. You're in

France! *Chil-dren, come!* I'll show you that French joie de vivre! * Par -

Tempo 1 ♩ = 88

is holds___ the key to___ your heart.

And all of___ Par - is plays___ a

* Pronounced "vee."

Paris Holds the Key - 11 - 2
0090B

* Pronounced "Moo-lan."

"Love Is A Journey We're

Only Beginning On...

Starting At The Beginning

With You"

As performed by Richard Marx and Donna Lewis

At The Beginning

Lyrics by LYNN AHRENS

Music by STEPHEN FLAHERTY

(with pedal)

Verse:

1. We were stran - gers start-ing out on a jour-ney, nev-er dream-ing what we'd

have to go through.___ Now here we are and I'm sud-den-ly stand - ing

At the Beginning - 7 - 1
0090B

"HOME, LOVE, FAMILY...

I WILL NEVER BE COMPLETE

UNTIL I FIND YOU"

As performed by Aaliyah

Journey To The Past

Lyrics by LYNN AHRENS

Music by STEPHEN FLAHERTY

Journey to the Past - 8 - 1
0090B

to the past.

Heart, don't fail me now.

Cour - age, don't de - sert me.

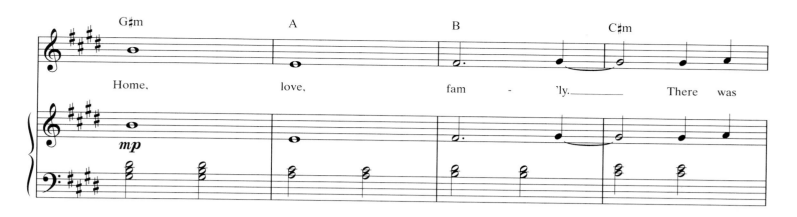

Home, love, fam - 'ly._____ There was

once a time__ I must have had_____ them, too._____

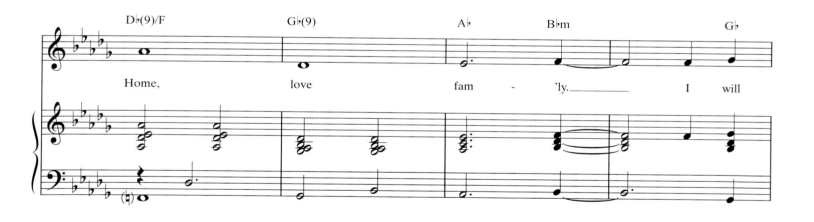

Home, love fam - 'ly._____ I will

nev - er be com - plete un - til I find you._____

80

Journey to the Past - 8 - 6
0090B

"En Algún Lugar Alguien Me Recuerda

Sueño Que Será Verdad."

As performed by Thalia

Viaje Tiempo Atras
(Journey To The Past)

Lyrics by LYNN AHRENS
Spanish Translation by PATRICIA P. AZAR
and EDUARDO GIACCARDO

Music by STEPHEN FLAHERTY

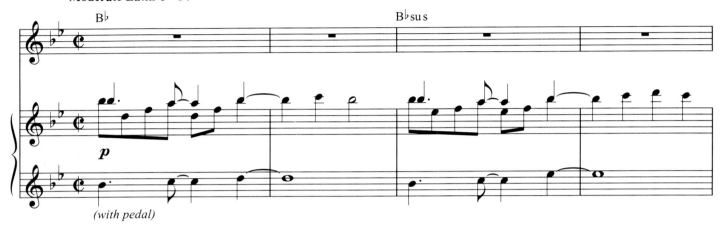

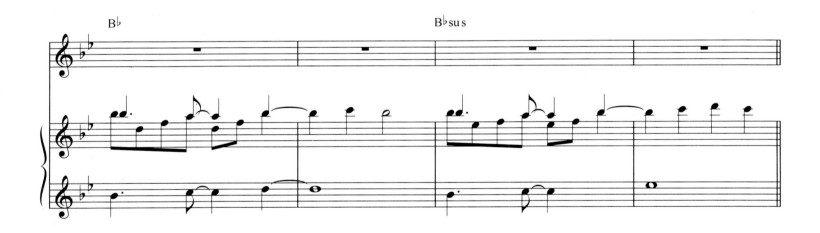

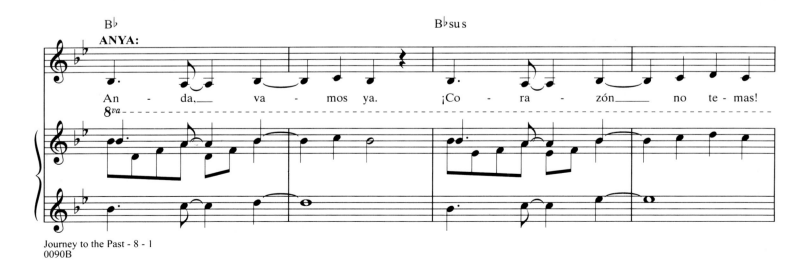

Journey to the Past - 8 - 1
0090B

ABOUT THE SONGWRITERS

LYNN AHRENS (LYRICS) AND STEPHEN FLAHERTY (MUSIC) ARE MEMBERS OF BROADWAY'S NEW GENERATION, A SONGWRITING TEAM IN THE TRADITION OF THE AMERICAN MUSICAL THEATRE'S FINEST COLLABORATIONS.

MOST RECENTLY, THEY WROTE THE SCORE FOR THE NEW MUSICAL "RAGTIME" (BASED ON THE E.L. DOCTOROW NOVEL, WITH BOOK BY TERRENCE MCNALLY, PRODUCED BY LIVENT, INC.), WHICH WAS NAMED THIS SEASON'S BEST MUSICAL FOR ITS WORLD PREMIERE IN TORONTO. A SECOND COMPANY OF "RAGTIME" PREMIERED IN LOS ANGELES AT THE SHUBERT THEATRE TO CRITICAL ACCLAIM, AND THE SHOW ARRIVES ON BROADWAY IN DECEMBER OF '97, WHERE IT WILL OPEN AT THE FORD CENTER FOR THE PERFORMING ARTS ON THE NEW 42ND STREET.

AHRENS AND FLAHERTY ARE THE CO-CREATORS OF THE HIT BROADWAY MUSICAL "ONCE ON THIS ISLAND," WHICH WAS AWARDED LONDON'S 1995 OLIVIER AWARD AS BEST MUSICAL, AND RECEIVED EIGHT TONY AWARD NOMINATIONS, NAACP THEATRE AWARDS FOR BEST MUSICAL AND BEST PLAYWRIGHT, AND DRAMA CRITICS CIRCLE AND OUTER CRITICS CIRCLE NOMINATIONS.

ALSO FOR BROADWAY, THEY WROTE THE SCORE FOR "MY FAVORITE YEAR," THE FIRST ORIGINAL AMERICAN MUSICAL EVER PRODUCED BY LINCOLN CENTER.

THEIR MUSICAL FARCE "LUCKY STIFF," FIRST PRODUCED OFF-BROADWAY BY PLAYWRIGHTS HORIZONS, WON THE PRESTIGIOUS RICHARD RODGERS AWARD AND WASHINGTON'S 1990 HELEN HAYES AWARD AS BEST MUSICAL.

INDIVIDUALLY, MS. AHRENS IS THE LYRICIST AND CO-BOOK WRITER FOR "A CHRISTMAS CAROL," MADISON SQUARE GARDEN'S ANNUAL HOLIDAY MUSICAL (WITH MUSIC BY ALAN MENKEN) NOW ENTERING ITS FOURTH SEASON IN NEW YORK. FOR HER WORK IN NETWORK TELEVISION AS A SONGWRITER, CREATOR AND PRODUCER, MS. AHRENS HAS RECEIVED THE EMMY AWARD AND FOUR EMMY NOMINATIONS AND HER SONGS ARE A MAINSTAY OF THE RENOWNED ANIMATED SERIES "SCHOOLHOUSE ROCK."

MR. FLAHERTY WROTE THE INCIDENTAL MUSIC FOR NEIL SIMON'S NEW PLAY "PROPOSALS," WHICH OPENED ON BROADWAY THIS YEAR. HE WAS ALSO RECENTLY COMMISSIONED TO WRITE AN ORCHESTRAL SUITE BASED ON THE MUSICAL THEMES OF "RAGTIME," WHICH PREMIERED ON THE FOURTH OF JULY AT THE HOLLYWOOD BOWL, AND HIS MUSICAL THEMES FROM "ANASTASIA" WERE FEATURED AT THE BOWL IN A "TRIBUTE TO THE MUSIC OF TWENTIETH CENTURY FOX." HE IS A FOUNDING MEMBER OF THE ACCLAIMED NEW THEATRE COMPANY, "DRAMA DEPT."

CAST RECORDINGS OF AHRENS AND FLAHERTY SHOWS ARE AVAILABLE ON RCA/VICTOR, SONY, TER AND VARESE SARABANDE.

THE SONG SCORE FOR TWENTIETH CENTURY FOX'S "ANASTASIA" MARKS THEIR MOTION PICTURE DEBUT.